How to Become a Successful Conference Speaker

Shawn Collins

Table of Contents

Who am I and What Do I Know About Speaking at Conferences?

Hi, I'm Shawn Collins, and I've been a speaker at conferences, seminars, and meet-ups consistently since 1999. I've been a solo speaker, panelist, moderator, emcee, and pretty much any other role where you stand up at a podium and speak to a crowd.

So, over all of these years, I've submitted many speaker proposals. A lot of them were accepted, and I've been on stage dozens of times.

I've also been turned down for many of my speaker proposals, so I've gotten a good sense for what does and does not appeal to conference organizers.

Also, I co-founded the Affiliate Summit conference in 2003, and I've handled the relationships with speakers since then.

This experience has given me an insider's view to all of the speaker proposals and feedback from the audience over more than a decade.

We started filming all of the educational sessions in 2006, so I like to watch the sessions with the audience feedback to get a clear view of why some speakers fall flat with the audience, while others connect and put on sensational sessions.

Now I am sharing my insight from this 360-degree view of speaking at conferences. If you are interested in becoming a conference speaker, or you've already done it, but you'd like to improve, I've compiled a bunch of tips and advice here to benefit you.

Introduction

There are many reasons to speak at conferences. In the early days of my career, it was all about money. My boss wasn't willing to pay for me to get a conference pass, but changed her tune when I was accepted for a speaking slot.

This scenario played itself out a few times before I really understood the benefits of speaking at a conference, and they were far greater than getting a comp pass to the event.

I first came to the realization that being a speaker gives back in a bunch of ways when I had my first book published, "Successful Affiliate Marketing for Merchants," back in 2001. Shortly after it came out, I was speaking at a conference and got permission to bring books to sell after my presentation.

I carried in 25 or so copies, and hoped I wouldn't be bringing them all back to my room afterwards. That didn't turn out to be an issue. They all sold, and a bunch of people still wanted to buy them.

That experience was informative in a couple of ways, as it helped me understand that speaking can have lots of indirect benefits. I would never sell from the stage, and the thing is it's not even necessary to do that.

Simply by sharing useful information and an excellent presentation, you are able to promote a book, site, personal brand, company, etc. without openly promoting, because people will read your bio to learn more about you.

Plus, it's a great way to give back to the industry when you share your knowledge, which earns you capital among people in your business. Not to mention that it's just supremely wonderful and fulfilling to help people.

Then there is the aspect of building up your own confidence and self-esteem among your peers. Let's face it, public speaking can be sort of scary, but the more you do it, the better you become, and that skill can be translated in all sorts of areas in your business and personal life.

Finally, when you take questions from the crowd, you may be challenged by what some folks have to say, and that can help to change your position, which can then benefit you, your site, company, or whatever.

Part 1: Making a Quality Speaker Proposal

There are dos and don'ts when it comes to submitting a speaker proposal. You only have one opportunity to make your case for speaking, so make the most of it.

Pay attention to the details and invest time in a quality speaker proposal.

Don't rush through it.

Typos, lack of clarity in your writing, and failing to follow the instructions send a very clear message that this is not a priority for you.

I'm guessing you don't want to send that message, since you're opting to read this book.

Based on the thousands of speaker proposals I've seen over the years, the pages that follow are my advice on what to do to improve your chances of being selected.

Read the Guidelines and Follow Them

This should be basic advice – so basic that it doesn't need to be included here.

However, every time we put out a call for speakers, I see lots of talented, successful people turn in proposals that show they've paid no attention to the guidelines.

If there are character or word constraints, be sure to adhere to them.

It's that simple.

Failure to follow simple instructions can disqualify a good session, so read the guidelines like they matter… because they do.

Check Your Schedule

Are you sure you do not have a conflict on your schedule with the conference day(s)?

Check and double check your schedule to see if you have any other obligations.

If you realize you have to cancel after being accepted to speak, it could hurt your credibility and cause trouble for the conference organizers.

Adhere to the Deadline

There is inevitably a deadline to turn in a speaker proposal. If you want to speak at a given conference, make it a priority to get the proposal in on time.

Lots of successive dates hinge on that deadline, and if that doesn't work for your schedule, so be it.

But your failure to meet the deadline is just that – your failure.

Don't Be Lazy

When you are submitting your speaker proposal, provide the requested information in full.

Don't cut corners with comments like "I will provide this later," because there will likely not be a later.

Exhibiting such arrogance, that you think the conference wants you to speak so bad that they'll accept your incomplete submission, may well result in your submission being declined.

Proofread!

There seems to be a theme here about attention to detail, right? Right.

Run spellcheck, read through your material for clarity, and have somebody else look it over before you send it.

People with typos on their resumes don't get hired.

Don't Be Too Broad

Are you one of those people who hopes to give a 30,000 foot view of your chosen topic?

If so, stop with the buzzwords and focus on a topic.

The big picture can be nice for a keynote, but if you're interested in giving a presentation at a breakout session, broad is bad. People want specifics.

Sell the Topic

Your speaker proposal should focus on the benefits, takeaways, etc. of your proposed session.

Don't talk about yourself. That is the function of your bio.

Review Past Agendas

One of the best ways to get a feel for the type of content that is typically featured at a conference is to review the past agendas.

Then, come up with a new, unique, interesting topic that draws some inspiration from past, recurring themes.

Don't Recycle

It's really nice to recycle paper, plastic, and grass clippings, but don't recycle content.

Nobody wants your greatest hits from the past few years. Respect your audience and propose new, quality content.

Focus on Clarity

Be clear about what you want to cover in your presentation. It should be something you can sum up in a sentence.

A string of buzzwords is annoying to read, has little meaning, and will likely help to put your proposal in the reject pile.

Have You Attended the Conference?

While there are certainly first timers speaking frequently at conferences, it is in your best interest to first attend conferences where you hope to speak at beforehand.

Know the conference culture and types of attendees, so you're not going into it blind.

Find Out What They Want

Do your homework as to which sessions have been most popular in the past, so you know what attendees like.

Also, read blog posts on the past conferences to gain insight.

Don't ask the organizers what they want – they want quality, original content.

Know Your Limits

It can be tough to carry an hour long session by yourself.

Are you ready? If not, try proposing for a shorter time slot, or submit a proposal for a panel.

Running a long session shouldn't be your first step. It's really helpful to get some experience by speaking at meet-ups and other smaller, professional get-togethers.

Part 2: After Being Accepted as a Speaker

So you passed the first test and your speaker proposal was accepted.

Now comes the real work. There are a lot of elements that go into a successful and interesting session. The process starts the day you are accepted to speak.

There are a lot of things you can do in advance, in addition to crafting great content, to ensure that you'll put on a quality session.

Get started on your presentation as soon as you are notified that you will be speaking, so you don't risk anything falling through the cracks.

Read the Speaker Agreement

The speaker agreement is a contract, and when you agree to it, you're agreeing to those terms and you are expected to abide by them.

Don't ask for extra perks – when you agree to speaker terms, read them.

If they say you don't get an extra pass for your boss, respect that and don't ask for a pass.

Don't ask for the slides to not be shared publicly if you've agreed to share them in the terms.

Promote Your Session

When you get the details on your session, let your friends and colleagues in your social networks know about it.

Mention the information in your blog and newsletter, put a plug in your email signature, too.

Some conferences have an affiliate program – join and use that link to promote your session.

Don't stop promoting. Most people don't promote their session at the conference. Stand out by giving people cards or flyers directing them to your session.

Set Up Tweets in Advance

People in your session will be feverishly writing the URLs of resources you mention.

Make it easier on them and schedule Tweets to drop during your session at the approximate time you are talking about them (you should have this down pretty close from practicing the session).

Also, include the room where you are speaking and the conference hashtag, so you can drum up more attendees in person.

Be sure to let the folks in the room know you are doing this, and you'll get new, engaged followers, too.

Practice Several Times

There are two types of speakers – those who practice, and those who make excuses about why their session was subpar.

Practice your talk three or four times, or more, so that you really have it down.

This will help you have a smoother delivery, and also ensure that you don't run out of your allotted time, which is very unfair to the next speaker.

Plus, you'll be more relaxed when you have mastered your material.

Get Changes Authorized

When your speaker proposal is accepted, the content delivered at the conference is expected to be the same as the conference posts on the official agenda.

Don't change the session title and/or description on your slides without getting it cleared with the conference first.

Otherwise, people will think they are in the wrong session if your slides and/or content are different from what is on the agenda.

Official Slide Template

If you are not sure whether there is a required template for slides from the conference, go ahead and ask.

This is important before doing your slides, because you don't want to find out that you'll have to change things to adhere to an official template.

Avoid Procrastination

When you get the deadlines, start planning around them. Don't wait until the last minute.

Organize your materials as early as possible. Don't miss deadlines – get your slides and other materials in on time, make A/V requests by the deadline.

If you put off things until the last minute, you and the audience will suffer.

K.I.S.S Your Slides

K.I.S.S. (keep it simple, stupid) your slides, because the more bells and whistles, such as video and audio, the better chance something won't work.

Also, sometimes the conference internet falls out at exactly the wrong time.

That's not to say you should go with this sort of media when it could enhance your presentation, but be sure to have a backup plan if the fancy stuff flames out.

Arrive Early to Prepare

Check the agenda and get over to the room for your session as soon as the previous session ends.

Take advantage of this time to verify the slides are there and working, the audio is good, etc.

This is also a good time to test the clicker, get mic'd up, and get familiar with the room, so you can start on time.

Plus, it is a good idea to introduce yourself to any show staff that are in the room, so you can communicate any important information to them.

Crank Up Your Energy and Passion

What is your key to getting amped up for a session... caffeine, music, chocolate? Have some of whatever your thing is, so you can hit the stage with passion and energy.

In the event that you're not feeling great for whatever reason, don't make excuses to the audience about why you are not 100%.

Saying things like "I'm tired" or "I'm hung-over" are very poor form – just give it your best.

Remember that people came to see you. They chose your session for a reason, so give it your best.

Have Fun

You should enjoy the experience of speaking at the conference.

Don't take yourself too seriously. Be informal and conversational. Nobody wants to see a professor up there.

Be the Content

You put together your slides – be sure to compile something you are proud to share.

Don't apologize for something being hard to read. Instead, use bigger fonts and less words. The words should be from your mouth, not on the screen.

Don't read your slides word for word – there is no use in you being there if you're doing that.

Economize on the words, so people are paying attention to you.

Know Your Audience

If you're not sure who is seated in front of you, ask them at the start of the session and adjust accordingly if they are more/less advanced.

This sort of interactive ice-breaker also serves to get their attention.

No Self-Promotion

Don't promote yourself or your product/service or company – let your knowledge sell you.

If you try to sell or promote, you run the risk of losing people's attention, and making people feel uncomfortable.

People can find more about you in your biography.

Have a Plan B

Sometimes you have to call an audible if the Internet, clicker, etc. doesn't work.

Don't throw conference organizers under the bus if something unexpected happens.

Instead, pivot and make it work.

Leave Time for Questions

It's better to have time for questions and get none than to run out of time and leave people hanging.

If there is an awkward period where nobody raises their hand with a question, have a few frequently asked questions ready to ask yourself and answer.

Repeat Audience Questions

When audience members do ask you a question, be sure to repeat those questions through the microphone, so the rest of the audience can hear it.

Some people will shout questions without a microphone and others simply don't project well, so it's important to re-share those questions with the audience before answering.

Don't Rush Out

Account for people talking to you after the session – people will typically want to chat with you. Don't bolt out of the room. Make yourself available even later on to have lunch, drinks, etc.

If you have to leave the room for the next speaker to get set up, announce to the audience that they can meet you in the hall or a specific location at the conference.

Also, don't be a diva that swoops in for their session and then takes off.

If you're so important that you can only make it to your session, and not the rest of the conference, you probably can't be missed from your office.

Network and learn – take advantage of the opportunity.

Thicken Your Skin

When you get feedback, you'll get some negative comments, even if you were outstanding.

Don't sweat it.

Instead, think about how you can address any issues that people bring up.

Sometimes, there will be unreasonable comments, and you just have to let it roll off you, because you can't please everybody.

Some Parting Words...

You will get turned down sometimes for speaking engagements. Everybody does. Don't obsess over it. Just pick up and move on. Feel free to ask the conference organizers why they didn't select you.

It may bruise your ego, but it will also make you better.

Be persistent – being turned down one time doesn't mean you will be turned next time.

Also, don't look at any speaking opportunity as too small for you. Start small by speaking at meet-ups and smaller conferences to build up a body of work.

You never know what any given speaking gig could propel you to in the future.

www.ingramcontent.com/pod-product-compliance
Lightning Source LLC
Chambersburg PA
CBHW071547170526
45166CB00004B/1578